My Human Being Owner's Manual

Knowing, Loving and Caring for Me

Pat Hansen
Co-Author: You!

Balboa Press books may be ordered through booksellers or by contacting:

Balboa Press
A Division of Hay House
1663 Liberty Drive
Bloomington, IN 47403
www.balboapress.com
844-682-1282

Print information available on the last page.

ISBN: 978-1-5043-4740-2 (sc)
ISBN: 978-1-5043-4742-6 (hc)
ISBN: 978-1-5043-4741-9 (e)

Library of Congress Control Number: 2016900237

Balboa Press rev. date: 06/06/2022

BALBOA.PRESS
A DIVISION OF HAY HOUSE

Dedicated to Alan's "Best Group Ever," and Alan.
Thank you for adding so much to my life.

TABLE OF CONTENTS

"Just be yourself.
There is no one better."

– Taylor Swift

Name:

Make: *Human Being*

Model: *Male*   *Female*

Ethnicity:

Year:

Hair Color:

Eye Color:

Other Features:

"When you change the
way you look at things,
the things you look
at change.

– Dr. Wayne Dyer

How it came about

I was 39 years old, married, healthy, and successful in a career as a graphic designer, traveling to great destinations with a beautiful new home that I shared with my husband. Over a period of time, I began to realize that I wasn't truly happy.

But why? I was relatively clueless.

Thus began an exploration of my unhappiness. As I spent time thinking about it, I realized that I just didn't feel fulfilled. I felt like there had to be something more, that something was missing. Everything I did seemed to be for someone else. I wasn't even sure what it was I WOULD do for myself if given the time. I didn't know what was absent in my life.

My design career dictated that I hone my skills as a problem solver and so, I decided to make this exploration a new project. The project was "ME." Getting to know myself, what made me tick, what my needs were, what was inside of me – the real, authentic me. Not the me that my design firm, clients, employees and peers needed me to be, not the wife my husband wanted me to be, not the daughter and sister my family expected me to be.

You might be thinking this was a selfish quest. Perhaps it was, but it was a quest that felt very necessary.

And so, I approached the project like I would any other – with research. I began by making a list of questions I wanted genuine answers to. I thought and thought and thought. I spent time alone. I searched my mind, my spirit, my soul. I added notes over the days and months, and soon I had quite a bit of knowledge of who I was – and who I wasn't – and who I wanted to be. Some of the findings were surprising, "aha" moments. Others were a bit scary in terms of how I was living life. But more than anything, I realized that what was forming before me was a set of guidelines, a reference manual, a collection of helpful information about myself. A go-to book for my life.

I remembered hearing the words "human beings don't come with owner's manuals." Inspired by this concept, I began expanding the idea with my own information – even referring to my car manual, refrigerator manual and others! You may laugh, but they were inspiring.

After some months, my finished document was designed, spiral bound, and ready for use.

My decision to share it with my husband of 15 years, who after nearly a year of my "unhappiness and selfishness" had most likely had enough – did not go as expected. When I shared the book, pouring myself on the table over breakfast, his first words were not "wow" or "cool" or "that's amazing." His first words were "I don't believe it."

Needless to say, I was stunned. How could he not believe what my soul had poured into these pages? What's not to believe?

Sadly, my marriage never recovered. While I gained a great deal of vision, confidence and ideas for living life forward, I lost something that was important to me. Looking back, I now know that I was set free to be me. Perhaps if both my husband and I had done this earlier, we could have adapted, accepted, or made a decision earlier. Hindsight!

My theory for *My Human Being Owner's Manual* is that if people took the time in their lives to get to know themselves as well as they do others, by creating a manual for themselves, it would benefit them greatly. They could be much happier and live more authentic lives. Because we all grow and evolve over time, an update yearly or at least every few years would keep it current. Sharing it with with others if appropriate – would make for improved relationships. Taking the time to really know oneself brings such clarity to life's challenges and decisions. I have found it to be the best gift to myself - ever.

If each of us had an owner's manual – I believe, we would be better equipped to be the best partners, parents, sisters, brothers we can possibly be – by understanding ourselves and others better. And, be much, much happier.

How I used my own

Once my owner's manual was complete, I immediately had a greater sense of who I was, what was important to me, what I enjoyed and what I didn't. I knew what I valued most in life, and knew to plan my life around those things. Knowing all of this, and referring back to the words I had written now and then – was tremendously helpful.

Probably most importantly, the knowledge helped me in making decisions – both large and small. Everything from work choices to friends, activities and vacation choices became easier to make. I discovered that one of my loves is being by water, especially the ocean. I know that it brings great calm to my spirit and provides time to think about the big picture. I learned that one of my priorities in life is being kind. I began practicing kindness every day – it didn't matter where I was – in a store, with new acquaintances, with someone in a bad mood. On the other hand, I found that I greatly dislike feeling out of control of my physical body. So I made the move from downhill skiing to cross country – more my speed!

In my friendships and work relationships, I was able to be clearer about not only my needs and opinions, but was also able to listen more carefully to theirs – without judgment. Opinions, yes, but only in the kindest of ways. I also knew that I valued honesty, loyalty, kindness, humor and intelligence. I didn't like loud, aggressive, angry or dishonest people. So I carefully worked my way around those types, not inviting a closer relationship into my life.

My actual work – that of a graphic design firm owner – was more rewarding in that the relationships were better with both employees and clients. I wasn't all over the map, but strong in my knowledge of the kind of work I wanted to pursue, and the kind of people I wanted to work with or hire. I was a better mentor, knowing the kinds of ways to help build a person's strengths. I became a better listener, knowing that each of us is unique, and there isn't one right way of thinking.

In potential relationships, I looked for kindness, humor, honesty, some sort of faith, happiness in their life, and work that they enjoyed doing. Granted I didn't always find all these things in potential partners, and made mistakes along the way, but inside I knew!

To get through difficult moods, I had my troubleshooting section. I knew things I could try to lift the mood, or pass the anger. I knew small things that made me happy. I knew ways to move around or through whatever was troubling me.

And most importantly, I knew what my life was about, what gifts I was given, what brought joy to my life. I was able to travel through the years with a great gift of knowledge about myself. And that helped me understand others, be more compassionate, and practice acceptance and kindness every day.

CHAPTER 1

Why Should You Have an Owner's Manual?

Have you ever bought a new piece of software, an appliance or an audio/video component that caused you to want to pull your hair out? Or have you had something stop working properly and gone to the owner's manual to troubleshoot ... and found something helpful? Or perhaps you have just bought a cool new gadget. Do you understand all of its capabilities or have you just tapped the surface?

The most complex "machinery" you will ever operate is your own self. Have you ever wondered about or wished for an owner's manual for your own self? How about for someone you love?

There are zillions of books and programs that look deeply into being human—your inner and outer personas and how they function. With all the different kinds of tools available today, you can track your fitness, your food intake, your daily activities and your travels. But what about the stuff inside, the characteristics and unique qualities you hold? What about your strengths and weaknesses, your likes and dislikes, your favorite this or that, your hopes and dreams?

What if you possessed an easy-to-understand set of guidelines about who you are as an individual, how you function and how you can use this knowledge to impact the overall quality of your life?

You came into the world being nothing but your natural self—perfect, pure, innocent. In a very short time, you began to be influenced, molded and instructed by others. Over the years, as you lived your daily life, you began to reflect what you were told.

If you have forgotten your true authentic self—even in a small way —it's doubtful you are operating at your best. This manual is designed to help you move toward a more fulfilled, enriched and meaningful life.

Things to ask yourself:

- What do you value most in life?

- Are you living in conflict with those things?

- Do you sometimes act a certain way to impress people you don't care about for reasons that really don't matter?

- Do you make decisions that end up being not in your best interest?

The value in knowing yourself

Simply put, you will be able to choose living each day true to you, which is the real meaning of success. Remember, you are fabulous because you are unique.

Once you know yourself, you will be aware of your values in life, your beliefs, your personality, your priorities, your moods, your habits, your magnificent body, your relationships and more.

You will know your strengths and weaknesses, your passions and fears, your desires and dreams. You will be aware of your eccentricities and idiosyncrasies, your likes and dislikes, and your tolerances and limitations.

Growing up and growing older does not mean you know yourself better. Not knowing yourself becomes obvious sooner or later. A quiet but real frustration might live in your heart. You may choose to live with it and ignore it—or you may choose to start getting to know yourself in order to live a more fulfilled, truer life.

Knowing yourself takes a conscious effort. Only you can create the knowledge with intention and purpose by creating your own *My Human Being Owner's Manual.*

CHAPTER 2

Human Being Parts Defined

Human beings come equipped not only with a mind, body and heart but also a spirit, soul and gut that speak to you, if you listen. Put all of these to work as you go forward in completing your owner's manual.

While there are thousands of theories, definitions and explanations for these parts, for the purposes of this owner's manual, here are a few guidelines for how to think about each:

Mind | brain

The part of you that enables you to be aware of the world and your experiences, to think and to feel; the faculty of consciousness and thought.
Brain, intelligence, intellect, thinking

Body | physical form

Your physical structure, including your bones, flesh and organs.
Figure, form, physical presence

Spirit | the real you

The Divine inside of you, what you arrived with when you were born. Spirit is who you are originally. Personality is derived from your spirit.
Personality, God within, the absolute all of life

Soul | manifestation of spirit

Your spirit's way of manifesting itself. Soul reflects the thoughts that are given to you by spirit.
Spirit's reflection, actions, manifestations

Gut | inner voice

The knowledge inside of you that is already there, what you already know instinctively.
Instinct, inner voice, intuition

Heart | emotions

The heart is the center of your thoughts and emotions, especially love or compassion.
Emotions, feelings, love, affection

PARTS DIAGRAM

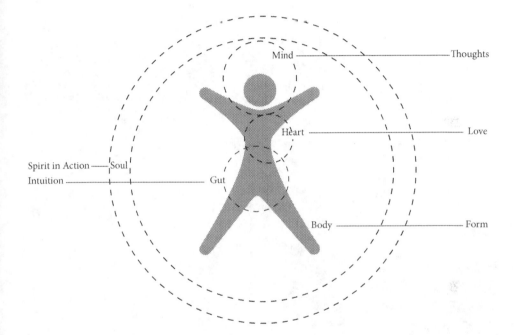

CHAPTER 3

Guidelines

The pages that follow are yours alone. Fill them in over a few days, a few months or longer. Go back and revisit the pages as often as you wish.

Here are some guidelines:

- Do your best. The more you give it, the more valuable it will be.

- These are your answers and yours alone.

- Listen to your gut, it speaks the truth.

- There are no wrong answers!

- If something doesn't apply to you, skip it.

- Be as honest as you can. Not everything you write will necessarily be positive.

- Take your time. There are no time limits. Take a day, a week or a year.

- Don't ask for others' opinions. This is you getting to know you.

- Use the last few pages to add anything else that wasn't covered in the provided pages.

- Use a pencil. You may want to go back and make adjustments.

- Have fun. You are getting to know the best you there is!

CHAPTER 4
Key Features

There are core values within you, beliefs and faith ideals, that are typically unbreakable. They don't change weekly, monthly or yearly. As life progresses sometimes they may shift in priority, or a new one may get added, but they are very steady.

These are the features about you that provide the foundation for your life. They help you to set priorities, make choices and live your life around them.

What is your foundation built upon?

My core values

Core values are the morals and principles you hold in your heart. They reside in your gut, and they rise up at all kinds of moments. In your work, in your home, in all aspects of your life, there are certain values you never want to compromise.

It's typical to have five to eight top values. Those values are put to use every day—as you make decisions, communicate with others, try to influence or persuade, encounter conflicts and engage in just about any other activity in life.

Values might include family, health, money, security, education, fun, innovation, faith—or a long list of other core principles might be at the top of your list.

What five to eight values are at the top of your list?

_____

_____

_____

_____

_____

_____

_____

_____

_____

_____

_____

_____

_____

_____

_____

_____

_____

_____

_____

_____

_____

_____

_____

_____

_____

Why are they important to you?

_____

_____

_____

_____

_____

_____

_____

_____

_____

_____

_____

_____

_____

_____

_____

_____

_____

_____

_____

_____

_____

_____

_____

_____

Are your values childhood carryovers, family influences, related to where you lived or live, where you went to school or the work you do?

_____

_____

_____

_____

_____

_____

_____

_____

_____

_____

_____

_____

_____

_____

_____

_____

_____

_____

_____

_____

_____

_____

Which two or three values are your top priorities?

_____

_____

_____

_____

_____

_____

_____

_____

_____

_____

_____

_____

_____

_____

_____

_____

_____

_____

_____

_____

_____

_____

_____

_____

_____

_____

Do you live up to them?

_____

_____

_____

_____

_____

_____

_____

_____

_____

_____

_____

_____

_____

_____

_____

_____

_____

_____

_____

_____

_____

_____

_____

_____

_____

_____

_____

_____

Do you feel you have to compromise?

_____

_____

_____

_____

_____

_____

_____

_____

_____

_____

_____

_____

_____

_____

_____

_____

_____

_____

_____

_____

_____

_____

_____

_____

_____

"To be yourself in a world that is constantly trying to make you something else is the greatest accomplishment."

– *Ralph Waldo Emerson*

My faith

Faith, for purposes here, is the ability to trust in something greater than yourself, from the very core of your being. You might have faith in the universe, God, a higher power or creation, or any one of many possibilities.

Faith in the universe as a whole might mean that you believe it's working on your behalf, not conspiring against you, not indifferent to you, but supporting you. Faith in God might be a belief in a Divine One. It might not be named God but as a supreme being or a higher power, or it might be known by another name.

Maybe you don't believe in any sort of higher power. If not, skip these pages or write about whatever you believe in.

What do you believe?

How do you describe your beliefs?

_____

_____

_____

_____

_____

_____

_____

_____

_____

_____

_____

_____

_____

_____

_____

_____

_____

_____

_____

_____

_____

_____

_____

_____

_____

_____

Do your beliefs impact your life, and how?

_____

_____

_____

_____

_____

_____

_____

_____

_____

_____

_____

_____

_____

_____

_____

_____

_____

_____

_____

_____

_____

_____

_____

_____

Are you tolerant of those whose beliefs differ from yours?

CHAPTER 5

Internal Operations

All the workings of mind, body and spirit bring out certain thoughts, attitudes and beliefs that you hold within and, most often, share with the world through your behavior.

Your personality, your moods, your habits and more, all come from your internal thought processes. Take some time to think about who you are as you answer the questions below.

What you think about yourself is most often a combination of positive and negative. There are probably some individuals who have achieved a more positive view of everything about themselves, but doubtfully 100 percent. If you can view the negatives as just less positive and perhaps something to work on, then you can begin to love yourself a little more.

My personality

Every human being has individual differences in behavior, thought, understanding and emotion. Maybe you are smart, outgoing and funny. Maybe you are compassionate, sincere and thoughtful. You definitely have your own ideas about who you are in your private moments as well as in your public ones.

You may be different in different environments. Or maybe you are even-keeled, not changing too much from one situation to another.

You likely know or hear the opinions of others, those around you. But what do you think about yourself, what do you know to be true?

How do you describe your personality?

What are you like on a good day?

_____

_____

_____

_____

_____

_____

_____

_____

_____

_____

_____

_____

_____

_____

_____

_____

_____

_____

_____

_____

_____

_____

_____

_____

_____

What are you like on a bad day?

_____

_____

_____

_____

_____

_____

_____

_____

_____

_____

_____

_____

_____

_____

_____

_____

_____

_____

_____

_____

_____

_____

_____

_____

_____

How are you at home?

_____

_____

_____

_____

_____

_____

_____

_____

_____

_____

_____

_____

_____

_____

_____

_____

_____

_____

_____

_____

_____

_____

How are you at work?

_____

_____

_____

_____

_____

_____

_____

_____

_____

_____

_____

_____

_____

_____

_____

_____

_____

_____

_____

_____

_____

_____

_____

_____

_____

"Be yourself; everyone else is already taken."

– *Oscar Wilde*

How are you with relatives?

How are you on vacation?

_____

_____

_____

_____

_____

_____

_____

_____

_____

_____

_____

_____

_____

_____

_____

_____

_____

_____

_____

_____

_____

_____

_____

How are you in social settings?

_____

_____

_____

_____

_____

_____

_____

_____

_____

_____

_____

_____

_____

_____

_____

_____

_____

_____

_____

_____

_____

_____

_____

_____

How are you with children?

_____
_____
_____
_____
_____
_____
_____
_____
_____
_____
_____
_____
_____
_____
_____
_____
_____
_____
_____
_____
_____
_____
_____
_____
_____

How are you with teenagers?

_____

_____

_____

_____

_____

_____

_____

_____

_____

_____

_____

_____

_____

_____

_____

_____

_____

_____

_____

_____

_____

_____

_____

_____

_____

_____

_____

_____

_____

How are you with people in your age group?

_____

_____

_____

_____

_____

_____

_____

_____

_____

_____

_____

_____

_____

_____

_____

_____

_____

_____

_____

_____

_____

_____

_____

_____

_____

"Always be a first-rate
version of yourself and not
a second-rate version
of someone else."

– *Judy Garland*

How are you with elderly people?

_____

_____

_____

_____

_____

_____

_____

_____

_____

_____

_____

_____

_____

_____

_____

_____

_____

_____

_____

_____

_____

_____

_____

_____

_____

How are you with people who differ greatly from you?

_____

_____

_____

_____

_____

_____

_____

_____

_____

_____

_____

_____

_____

_____

_____

_____

_____

_____

_____

_____

_____

_____

_____

_____

_____

How are you with people whom you don't like?

_____

_____

_____

_____

_____

_____

_____

_____

_____

_____

_____

_____

_____

_____

_____

_____

_____

_____

_____

_____

_____

_____

_____

Is there anything you would like to change about how you are with a certain type of person or people?

_____

_____

_____

_____

_____

_____

_____

_____

_____

_____

_____

_____

_____

_____

_____

_____

_____

_____

_____

_____

_____

_____

_____

_____

How could you go about making that change?

_____

_____

_____

_____

_____

_____

_____

_____

_____

_____

_____

_____

_____

_____

_____

_____

_____

_____

_____

_____

_____

_____

_____

_____

My moods

Your moods are the emotional state you feel at given times. It's not possible to be in the same mood 100 percent of the time. In the simplest of terms, moods are said to be good or bad, but in fact there are many places in between. Moods are generally not long-lasting, but temporary.

You may be happy, sad, depressed, exhausted or energized. You may feel inferior or superior.

On an average basis, what are you like when you wake up?

_____

_____

_____

_____

_____

_____

_____

_____

_____

_____

_____

_____

_____

_____

_____

_____

_____

_____

_____

_____

_____

_____

_____

_____

_____

What are you like as you move through a typical day?

_____

_____

_____

_____

_____

_____

_____

_____

_____

_____

_____

_____

_____

_____

_____

_____

_____

_____

_____

_____

_____

_____

_____

_____

_____

_____

_____

What are you like during a typical evening?

_____

_____

_____

_____

_____

_____

_____

_____

_____

_____

_____

_____

_____

_____

_____

_____

_____

_____

_____

_____

_____

_____

_____

What do you consider to be your best time of day?

_____

_____

_____

_____

_____

_____

_____

_____

_____

_____

_____

_____

_____

_____

_____

_____

_____

_____

_____

_____

_____

_____

_____

_____

What types of things make you feel loving?

_____

_____

_____

_____

_____

_____

_____

_____

_____

_____

_____

_____

_____

_____

_____

_____

_____

_____

_____

_____

_____

_____

_____

_____

"To love yourself right now, just as you are, is to give yourself heaven. Don't wait until you die. If you wait, you die now. If you love, you live now."

– Alan Cohen

What types of things cause you to get angry?

_____

_____

_____

_____

_____

_____

_____

_____

_____

_____

_____

_____

_____

_____

_____

_____

_____

_____

_____

_____

_____

_____

_____

What types of things frustrate you?

_____

_____

_____

_____

_____

_____

_____

_____

_____

_____

_____

_____

_____

_____

_____

_____

_____

_____

_____

_____

_____

_____

_____

_____

_____

_____

What kinds of things cause stress?

_____

_____

_____

_____

_____

_____

_____

_____

_____

_____

_____

_____

_____

_____

_____

_____

_____

_____

_____

_____

_____

_____

What other moods do you have frequently, and what brings them on?

_____

_____

_____

_____

_____

_____

_____

_____

_____

_____

_____

_____

_____

_____

_____

_____

_____

_____

_____

_____

_____

_____

_____

_____

_____

_____

"The trick is to be grateful when your mood is high, and graceful when it is low."

– *Richard Carlson*

Are there any mood behaviors you want to change?

_____

_____

_____

_____

_____

_____

_____

_____

_____

_____

_____

_____

_____

_____

_____

_____

_____

_____

_____

_____

_____

_____

_____

_____

_____

How might you go about changing them?

_____

_____

_____

_____

_____

_____

_____

_____

_____

_____

_____

_____

_____

_____

_____

_____

_____

_____

_____

_____

_____

_____

_____

My body image

Your physical presence is the "house" you live in. The "packaging" around what's inside. In scientific terms, your body is the entire structure that comprises a head, neck, trunk, arms and hands, legs and feet. At a cellular level, the average mature human being has the estimated average number of 37.2 trillion cells!

Your body image is thought to be, in part, a product of your personal experiences, personality, social and cultural forces. Your initial sense about your physical appearance may be a result of some cultural ideal. Your honest perception of your appearance will be different from that, or how others actually perceive you.

How would you describe your body image?

_____

_____

_____

_____

_____

_____

_____

_____

_____

_____

_____

_____

_____

_____

_____

_____

_____

_____

_____

_____

_____

_____

_____

_____

What do you love about it?

_____

_____

_____

_____

_____

_____

_____

_____

_____

_____

_____

_____

_____

_____

_____

_____

_____

_____

_____

_____

_____

_____

_____

_____

_____

_____

_____

What do you dislike?

"We're all entitled to our likes and dislikes. Imagine the world if we all liked the same things."

– *Malea Ann Haberman*

Do you often compare your body to the way it used to be?

Do you dream about what you would like it to be?

_____

_____

_____

_____

_____

_____

_____

_____

_____

_____

_____

_____

_____

_____

_____

_____

_____

_____

stronger,
bigger, smaller,
taller, shorter, cuter

_____

_____

_____

_____

What are you prepared to do to move toward that dream?

_____

_____

_____

_____

_____

_____

_____

_____

_____

_____

_____

_____

_____

_____

_____

_____

_____

_____

_____

_____

_____

_____

_____

My health

Your health is an overview of your physical, mental and social well-being. It's not simply about disease or the absence thereof. There are many influencing factors when it comes to health—lifestyle, environment and genetics to name a few.

Maximizing your level of health and wellness will help you to live a long, full and healthy life. The pursuit of health, personal growth and improved quality of life relies on living a balanced life.

If any of these three areas—physical, mental or social—is consistently lacking or forgotten about, you will not be at your optimal level of health. How is your health?

What do you believe about your mental health?

_____

_____

_____

_____

_____

_____

_____

_____

_____

_____

_____

_____

_____

_____

_____

_____

_____

_____

_____

_____

_____

_____

_____

What do you know about your physical body health?

_____

_____

_____

_____

_____

_____

_____

_____

_____

_____

_____

_____

_____

_____

_____

_____

_____

_____

_____

_____

_____

_____

_____

_____

_____

"You can discover more about a person in an hour of play than in a year of conversation."

– *Plato*

What do you feel about your social health – how you get along with other people, how other people react to you and how you interact with society?

_____

_____

_____

_____

_____

_____

_____

_____

_____

_____

_____

_____

_____

_____

_____

_____

_____

_____

_____

_____

_____

_____

Do you ignore or worry about any of the issues above?

_____

_____

_____

_____

_____

_____

_____

_____

_____

_____

_____

_____

_____

_____

_____

_____

_____

_____

_____

_____

_____

_____

_____

_____

Are there behaviors you could alter or add to achieve better
overall health?

Do you need support? What kind? Are you willing?

_____

_____

_____

_____

_____

_____

_____

_____

_____

_____

_____

_____

_____

_____

_____

_____

_____

_____

_____

_____

_____

_____

_____

_____

_____

My good habits

A habit is something you do regularly or repeatedly. Good habits are behaviors that benefit you and/or others in some way.

Good habits play a role in so many aspects of your well-being (both physical and mental) that you hold them as worth keeping or pursuing. Habits take a while to form and take a while to stick.

What habits are you committed to that you know are beneficial?

_____

_____

_____

_____

_____

_____

_____

_____

_____

_____

_____

_____

_____

_____

_____

_____

_____

_____

_____

_____

_____

_____

_____

Are there any old habits that you need to reinstate?

_____

_____

_____

_____

_____

_____

_____

_____

_____

_____

_____

_____

_____

_____

_____

_____

_____

_____

_____

_____

_____

_____

_____

Are there any new habits you would you like to adopt?

_____

_____

_____

_____

_____

_____

_____

_____

_____

_____

_____

_____

_____

_____

_____

_____

_____

_____

_____

_____

_____

_____

_____

_____

_____

"Your net worth to the world is usually determined by what remains after your bad habits are subtracted from your good ones."

– *Benjamin Franklin*

My not-so-good habits

Let's face it—we all do things that are not beneficial to us and/or others in some way.

A not-so-good habit is a negative behavior pattern. It might be something like being chronically late, fidgeting, procrastination, spending too much money or biting your nails.

A key factor in distinguishing a bad habit from an addiction (which we are not addressing here) is the element of will power. If you still seem to have some control over the behavior, then it's just a habit.

What is your number one not-so-good habit?

What are other not-so-good habits?

_____

_____

_____

_____

_____

_____

_____

_____

_____

_____

_____

_____

_____

_____

_____

_____

_____

_____

_____

_____

_____

_____

_____

_____

_____

How do the not-so-good habits make you feel?

_____

_____

_____

_____

_____

_____

_____

_____

_____

_____

_____

_____

_____

_____

_____

_____

_____

_____

_____

_____

_____

_____

_____

_____

_____

_____

"To improve is to change; to be perfect is to change often."

– *Winston Churchill*

Do you want to change any of them, and what can you do? Are you willing?

_____

_____

_____

_____

_____

_____

_____

_____

_____

_____

_____

_____

_____

_____

_____

_____

_____

_____

_____

_____

_____

_____

_____

_____

_____

_____

_____

My strengths

Your capacity to do something well, whether it's mental, physical or creative, is your strength.

When you try to determine your own strengths, think about what comes naturally easy for you—that probably isn't so easy for everyone else. Think of the strengths that describe your core being. What is so obvious that you almost don't notice it in yourself anymore, because it has become a part of your very nature?

If you focus on your strengths to the fullest, that is where you will find your competitive advantage and where you can create the most value for other people. Knowing your strengths and weaknesses raises your self-awareness and gives you clarity.

What do you consider to be your topmost strength?

What other strengths do you feel are a part of you?

Are any of these strengths something you would like to build upon?
Which ones, and how could you go about it?

_____

_____

_____

_____

_____

_____

_____

_____

_____

_____

_____

_____

_____

_____

_____

_____

_____

_____

_____

_____

_____

_____

_____

_____

_____

_____

_____

Are there strengths you would like to have or that you admire in others?

"Concentrate on your strengths, instead of your weaknesses...on your powers, instead of your problems."

– *Paul J. Meyer*

Are there things you could do to attain them?

_____

_____

_____

_____

_____

_____

_____

_____

_____

_____

_____

_____

_____

_____

_____

_____

_____

_____

_____

_____

_____

_____

_____

_____

My weaknesses

Are there things about your self that you feel are a little inadequate or weak? Maybe you have a tendency to be a little too much this or too much that? Or are there things that you believe you can't do?

Equally important to knowing what your personal strengths are is knowing your personal weaknesses. These are the skills or attributes that you have a hard time with, things you consider to be difficult or even impossible. Sometimes it helps just to recognize them as not being in your skillset and let someone else do them!

Everybody has weaknesses. It's a natural thing, humans are not perfect. So don't be embarrassed to look at your weaknesses. It will help you to improve in those areas or just choose to accept them.

What do you consider to be your top weakness?

_____

_____

_____

_____

_____

_____

_____

_____

_____

_____

_____

_____

_____

_____

_____

_____

_____

_____

_____

_____

_____

_____

_____

_____

_____

What other weaknesses do you feel you have?

_____

_____

_____

_____

_____

_____

_____

_____

_____

_____

_____

_____

_____

_____

_____

_____

_____

_____

_____

_____

_____

_____

_____

_____

Are there any weaknesses that you want to change?

_____

_____

_____

_____

_____

_____

_____

_____

_____

_____

_____

_____

_____

_____

_____

_____

_____

_____

_____

_____

_____

_____

_____

_____

How would you change them?

_____

_____

_____

_____

_____

_____

_____

_____

_____

_____

_____

_____

_____

_____

_____

_____

_____

_____

_____

_____

_____

_____

_____

_____

_____

_____

CHAPTER 6

Loves and Hates, Likes and Dislikes

Every day there are things, people, places and events happening all around you. Being aware of which of those you like and those you don't might seem like a simple task—but knowing this about yourself, and letting others close to you know, helps build a great definition of who you are.

So many of us go through life following what's popular, doing what others tell us, disliking what others dislike, etc. Be yourself, not a follower.

You and you alone get to decide. No one else gets a say in your list.

It might be difficult to record some of these realizations; it might seem odd or impolite. But honesty is the best policy here! If you keep being dragged into things you don't like and neglect what brings you joy, you are not only frustrated—you give up part of who you are.

Things I love

As you have lived your life, you have amassed a large number of things you like a lot—or things you absolutely love. Whether it's a person, place or thing, an idea, a fact or an attitude, you truly enjoy it.

These are the things you seek out, ask for and engage in regularly. They are things from your past, your present and perhaps your future. Often, our best memories are made from things we love.

I love

_____

_____

_____

_____

_____

_____

_____

_____

_____

_____

_____

_____

_____

_____

_____

_____

_____

_____

_____

_____

_____

_____

_____

_____

I like

"The firmest friendship
is based on an identity of likes
and dislikes."

– Sallust

Things I don't like

Like the things you love or like a lot, there are probably a number of things you don't like, or in fact even hate. These can be a person, place or thing, an idea, a fact or an attitude, or whatever pops into your head.

Similar to the like/love list, these things can make memories that you would rather not have. Knowing what stirs this negativity within you often helps you to avoid them in the future, or at least prepare yourself in advance in order to handle them.

I hate

_____

_____

_____

_____

_____

_____

_____

_____

_____

_____

_____

_____

_____

_____

_____

_____

_____

_____

_____

_____

_____

_____

_____

_____

_____

I dislike

_____

_____

_____

_____

_____

_____

_____

_____

_____

_____

_____

_____

_____

_____

_____

_____

_____

_____

_____

_____

_____

_____

_____

_____

CHAPTER 7

The Good and the Bad

Things that make me happy

Many of us probably don't feel a need to have a formal definition of happiness; it's just something we experience. We often use the word to describe how we are feeling at a given time. Happiness is typically the experiencing of positive emotions, including joy, pride, contentment and gratitude.

Certain events, people or things make you smile. They make you feel good inside. You want more of those moments, more of those days and more of those years.

Were there times in your life when you feel you were the happiest?

_____

_____

_____

_____

_____

_____

_____

_____

_____

_____

_____

_____

_____

_____

_____

_____

_____

_____

_____

_____

_____

_____

_____

_____

_____

What about those times do you think made you happy?

"Happiness is not something ready made. It comes from your own actions."

– *Dalai Lama*

What makes you happy in your current life?

_____

_____

_____

_____

_____

_____

_____

_____

_____

_____

_____

_____

_____

_____

_____

_____

_____

_____

_____

_____

_____

_____

What would make you happier?

_____

_____

_____

_____

_____

_____

_____

_____

_____

_____

_____

_____

_____

_____

_____

_____

_____

_____

_____

_____

_____

_____

_____

_____

What feeling(s) would you have if you attained the above?

Is there another way to gain the feeling(s) without attaining it?

Things I have accomplished

An accomplishment might be something you've done or something you've successfully achieved—large or small. You feel good about it when you think about the path you took to get there.

A memorable achievement might be deeply personal or it might have been publicly celebrated. The feelings that come from either are remarkably the same.

What have you achieved in your life that you feel good about?

Do you celebrate that accomplishment? How?

_____

_____

_____

_____

_____

_____

_____

_____

_____

_____

_____

_____

_____

_____

_____

_____

_____

_____

_____

_____

_____

_____

Do you have a "new" something in mind that you want to accomplish?

What are the steps you can take to accomplish it?

_____

_____

_____

_____

_____

_____

_____

_____

_____

_____

_____

_____

_____

_____

_____

_____

_____

_____

_____

_____

_____

_____

Things I have failed at

Failure comes in all sizes and degrees. Some are big and some are small, some might be clearly labeled failure, others not so much. It's a tough word, but how you move past it is what counts.

Do you have something you consider to be your greatest failure?

_____

_____

_____

_____

_____

_____

_____

_____

_____

_____

_____

_____

_____

_____

_____

_____

_____

_____

_____

_____

_____

_____

_____

_____

_____

How did it make you feel, and how long did you feel that way?

_____

_____

_____

_____

_____

_____

_____

_____

_____

_____

_____

_____

_____

_____

_____

_____

_____

_____

_____

_____

_____

_____

_____

_____

_____

"I can accept failure,
everyone fails at
something. But I can't
accept not trying."

– *Michael Jordan*

Were you able to recover, pick up the pieces and move on? How?

What did you learn?

Do any smaller failures come to mind?

_____

_____

_____

_____

_____

_____

_____

_____

_____

_____

_____

_____

_____

_____

_____

_____

_____

_____

_____

_____

_____

_____

_____

_____

What did you learn from them?

Things that make me sad

Sadness is a heavy-heartedness that hurts deep inside. It may come upon you by feeling disadvantage, loss, helplessness or disappointment.

You might become sad because your expectations weren't met. You expected a certain outcome from an event, a person or a thing and it did not happen. You didn't anticipate the possibility of it not working or happening, and you get hit by the outcome.

During these times, you may react in different ways—you may become quiet, lethargic or withdraw yourself from others. You might cry endlessly.

Are there things from your childhood that make you sad?

_____

_____

_____

_____

_____

_____

_____

_____

_____

_____

_____

_____

_____

_____

_____

_____

_____

_____

_____

_____

_____

_____

_____

_____

What about while you were growing up?

_____

_____

_____

_____

_____

_____

_____

_____

_____

_____

_____

_____

_____

_____

_____

_____

_____

_____

_____

_____

_____

_____

_____

_____

_____

_____

What makes you sad now?

_____

_____

_____

_____

_____

_____

_____

_____

_____

_____

_____

_____

_____

_____

_____

_____

_____

_____

_____

_____

_____

_____

_____

_____

_____

"The word happy would lose its meaning if it were not balanced by sadness."

– *Carl Jung*

What do you do when you are sad?

_____

_____

_____

_____

_____

_____

_____

_____

_____

_____

_____

_____

_____

_____

_____

_____

_____

_____

_____

_____

_____

_____

_____

Things that make me angry

You know that feeling you get sometimes. It can be sudden, in reaction to something or someone, or it can build over time. It's what you feel when someone is behaving poorly or something happens that enrages you. Whether it's a bad driver on the freeway or someone across from you at dinner that provokes it, anger is an intense emotional response.

Being aware of things, situations or people that often anger you can help you build up strength to react in a different manner because you are prepared, or help you avoid those things entirely. Anger can be detrimental to your overall health in many ways.

What makes you angry?

_____

_____

_____

_____

_____

_____

_____

_____

_____

_____

_____

_____

_____

_____

_____

_____

_____

_____

_____

_____

_____

_____

_____

_____

_____

_____

"When angry count to ten before you speak. If very angry, count to one hundred."

– *Thomas Jefferson*

How do you react? Do you hold onto it or let it out?

_____

_____

_____

_____

_____

_____

_____

_____

_____

_____

_____

_____

_____

_____

_____

_____

_____

_____

_____

_____

_____

_____

_____

_____

_____

How might you react differently to things that anger you?

_____

_____

_____

_____

_____

_____

_____

_____

_____

_____

_____

_____

_____

_____

_____

_____

_____

_____

_____

_____

_____

_____

_____

Things I fear

Fear is an unpleasant emotion caused by the belief that someone or something is dangerous, likely to cause pain or is a threat. It's a feeling of distress at the thought of something or a certain situation.

Fear is an emotion induced by some type of perceived or real threat that causes a change in thinking and sometimes bodily function. It often causes a change in behavior, such as hiding, running away or freezing up. Fear may take over in response to a specific current happening or to a future situation, which is perceived as a risk to health or life, status, power, security or, in the case of humans, anything that is valued.

What is your worst fear?

_____

_____

_____

_____

_____

_____

_____

_____

_____

_____

_____

_____

_____

_____

_____

_____

_____

_____

_____

_____

_____

_____

_____

_____

_____

_____

What else are you afraid of?

_____

_____

_____

_____

_____

_____

_____

_____

_____

_____

_____

_____

_____

_____

_____

_____

_____

_____

_____

_____

_____

_____

_____

Are there fears from your past that you have overcome?

_____

_____

_____

_____

_____

_____

_____

_____

_____

_____

_____

_____

_____

_____

_____

_____

_____

_____

_____

_____

_____

_____

_____

_____

_____

Do you want to overcome any fears you still have? How could you do that?

_____

_____

_____

_____

_____

_____

_____

_____

_____

_____

_____

_____

_____

_____

_____

_____

_____

_____

_____

_____

_____

_____

_____

_____

Things that bring me peace

We all need peace in our lives. It's that feeling of freedom from disturbing things—an overall sense of quiet and tranquility. It's a calmness that surrounds you, that makes you feel free and in harmony.

"Better than a thousand
hollow words, is one word that
brings peace."

– Buddha

What are some of the things or thoughts that bring you a sense
of peace?

_____

_____

_____

_____

_____

_____

_____

_____

_____

_____

_____

_____

_____

_____

_____

_____

_____

_____

_____

_____

_____

_____

_____

_____

_____

_____

What are some of your practices that bring you a sense of peace?

Are there certain places that bring you a sense of peace?

_____

_____

_____

_____

_____

_____

_____

_____

_____

_____

_____

_____

_____

_____

_____

_____

_____

_____

_____

_____

_____

_____

_____

_____

_____

_____

CHAPTER 8

Influences

In a typical lifetime, we meet people that have impacted us in a positive way. A teacher, an author, a parent, a lecturer or a celebrity – any one has the potential to inspire or influence you in a good way.

Sometimes the influence comes from someone we know well, but sometimes it is from someone we have never met. Whichever it might be, the results have stayed with you over time. You may live or strive to live by their words or philosophies, you may have learned something that has helped you through life, or you may have simply been in awe of what they have accomplished and admire it greatly.

Think about the people in your life.

Who has played a positive role in the life you are living?

Do you have someone you admire greatly? Why?

_____

_____

_____

_____

_____

_____

_____

_____

_____

_____

_____

_____

_____

_____

_____

_____

_____

_____

_____

_____

_____

_____

_____

_____

_____

_____

_____

Have you ever had (or do you have) a mentor?

_____

_____

_____

_____

_____

_____

_____

_____

_____

_____

_____

_____

_____

_____

_____

_____

_____

_____

_____

_____

_____

_____

_____

_____

_____

_____

Who in your life has (or had) the greatest positive influence on you?

_____

_____

_____

_____

_____

_____

_____

_____

_____

_____

_____

_____

_____

_____

_____

_____

_____

_____

_____

_____

_____

_____

_____

_____

How did this person (or people) inspire you?

Is there a person you would like to meet someday? Why?

"This above all: to thine own self be true."

– William Shakespeare

Has anyone ever given you some advice or words of wisdom that stayed with you? What were they?

Do you have a favorite quote or quotes?

CHAPTER 9

Preferences

Every person has certain things that they are attracted to. How this comes about is highly personal, no one can make you like or love something you don't. Your preferences make you more unique.

Sharing these things with others who enjoy them makes life fun. Sharing with others also helps them to know you better—all the better at gift giving time! And, sometimes sharing something new might get added to your list!

Take some time to be specific about your favorite things.

Colors: List some of your favorite colors, your go-to colors for clothes, cars, interiors and more.

Places: Where do you love to be—whether local or afar, a place, a restaurant, a city or a massage table:

_____

_____

_____

_____

_____

_____

_____

_____

_____

_____

_____

_____

_____

_____

_____

_____

_____

_____

_____

_____

_____

_____

_____

_____

Foods: Everyone has favorite tastes, what are yours?

_____

_____

_____

_____

_____

_____

_____

_____

_____

_____

_____

_____

_____

_____

_____

_____

_____

_____

_____

_____

_____

_____

_____

_____

_____

Books: If you like to read, what are some of your favorites?

TV shows: What are your all-time favorite TV shows?

_____

_____

_____

_____

_____

_____

_____

_____

_____

_____

_____

_____

_____

_____

_____

_____

_____

_____

_____

_____

_____

_____

_____

_____

Movies: What are your all-time favorite movies?

Music: What is your favorite music?

Sports: What are your favorite sports or activities?

_____

_____

_____

_____

_____

_____

_____

_____

_____

_____

_____

_____

_____

_____

_____

_____

_____

_____

_____

_____

_____

_____

_____

_____

_____

_____

_____

"My favorite things in life don't cost any money. It's really clear that the most precious resource we all have is time."

– *Steve Jobs*

Things: What are some of your favorite things that you collect or just love (like rocks, shells, cars, jewelry)?

CHAPTER 10
Dreams and Desires

Your hopes and dreams are the foundation of your future. Being aware of where you want to go in life and what you want to do will help you design the path forward.

Don't let anyone tell you that your dreams are unimportant—or that they don't matter. They do!

If you want to become a watercolor painter, ask yourself: What do you want to paint? What do you need to learn? Do you want painting to be a big part of your life or just a part-time hobby? The more you can define where you want to go, the more you will be able to make a plan.

Knowledge leads to action. Just being aware of something brings it forward in your conscience. Make your dreams part of your daily pursuits.

When you close your eyes and imagine doing exactly what you want, going exactly where you want to go, what do you think of?

What do you want in life?

What do you wish for in your own life?

_____

_____

_____

_____

_____

_____

_____

_____

_____

_____

_____

_____

_____

_____

_____

_____

_____

_____

_____

_____

_____

_____

_____

_____

What steps can you take to fulfill those wishes?

What do you wish for in your community?

_____

_____

_____

_____

_____

_____

_____

_____

_____

_____

_____

_____

_____

_____

_____

_____

_____

_____

_____

_____

_____

_____

_____

What are you willing to do to help make that happen?

_____

_____

_____

_____

_____

_____

_____

_____

_____

_____

_____

_____

_____

_____

_____

_____

_____

_____

_____

_____

_____

_____

_____

_____

What do you wish for in your country?

_____

_____

_____

_____

_____

_____

_____

_____

_____

_____

_____

_____

_____

_____

_____

_____

_____

_____

_____

_____

_____

_____

_____

What are you willing to do to help make that happen?

"...Ask not what your country can do for you, ask what you can do for your country."

– *John F. Kennedy*

What do you wish for in the world?

What are you willing to do to help make that happen?

_____

_____

_____

_____

_____

_____

_____

_____

_____

_____

_____

_____

_____

_____

_____

_____

_____

_____

_____

_____

_____

_____

_____

_____

Before you leave this earth, what do you want? Here's your chance to create a bucket list and then get to work on making it happen.

CHAPTER 11

Relationships

Unless you have chosen to live alone on a remote mountainside, you will often find yourself surrounded by others—out in public, at work and even at home. Human beings are often shaped in part by their relations to others.

How you interact with each person defines that relationship. This interaction is not always verbal, it might be physical, emotional or mental.

Relationships with other people are "alive" in that they change continuously during their existence. They usually grow and most often improve over time, as people get to know each other and become closer emotionally. Sometimes however, they fall apart as people choose to go their own ways—moving on with their lives and forming new relationships with others.

What are some of the qualities you most appreciate in
your friends?

What do you bring to your friendships?

What are the things that your family members (no matter how you define your family) add to your life that you are most thankful for?

What do you bring to your relationships with family?

There are certain traits and behaviors that your actual or preferred partner in life would have. Which are the most important to you?

What do you bring to a partnership?

_____

_____

_____

_____

_____

_____

_____

_____

_____

_____

_____

_____

_____

_____

_____

_____

_____

_____

_____

_____

_____

_____

_____

_____

_____

There are certain traits and behaviors that you want your peers and workmates to have. Which are the most important to you?

What do you bring to a work relationship?

CHAPTER 12

Troubleshooting

All humans encounter times of difficulty, times of trouble—which in turn causes undesirable moods or reactions.

Use this section to record any measures you've taken, or could take, to help remedy or change your thinking.

When I am feeling blue: When you are a bit down, there are things you can do (or someone can do for you) that always pick you up. Knowing how to lift your spirit is invaluable. What are some of the things that help?

_____

_____

_____

_____

_____

_____

_____

_____

_____

_____

_____

_____

_____

_____

_____

_____

_____

_____

_____

_____

_____

_____

"Sweet is the memory
of past troubles."

– Marcus Tullius Cicero

When I am feeling overwhelmed: When there is just too much
going on, too much on your to-do list, too much in general, it's a
good idea to know what will bring your calm back. What are some
things that help?

_____

_____

_____

_____

_____

_____

_____

_____

_____

_____

_____

_____

_____

_____

_____

_____

_____

_____

_____

_____

_____

_____

When I am sad: Sadness happens to all of us. Knowing what helps get you through, helps unburden the load, even if something small, helps. Try:

_____

_____

_____

_____

_____

_____

_____

_____

_____

_____

_____

_____

_____

_____

_____

_____

_____

_____

_____

_____

_____

_____

When I am frustrated: When you are filled with frustration,
and stress is beginning to win, these are some of the things that
will help;

When I am stressed: When you are filled with angst, and stress is consuming your body and mind, these are some of the things that will help you unwind:

_____

_____

_____

_____

_____

_____

_____

_____

_____

_____

_____

_____

_____

_____

_____

_____

_____

_____

_____

_____

_____

_____

_____

_____

When I am angry: There are times that cause every human being to get annoyed, mad or angry. What things come to mind that calm you down, help you settle yourself and help you work through it rather than letting it fester?

_____

_____

_____

_____

_____

_____

_____

_____

_____

_____

_____

_____

_____

_____

_____

_____

_____

_____

_____

_____

_____

_____

When I am hard on myself: We all can be our own worst critics. What can you do or think about to help you lighten up and love yourself as you are?

_____

_____

_____

_____

_____

_____

_____

_____

_____

_____

_____

_____

_____

_____

_____

_____

_____

_____

_____

_____

_____

_____

When I am sick: Every now and then we are going to get sick—with a cold, the flu or something else. What do you like to do for yourself when you don't feel well? What do you like others to do?

When I am tired: Whether your mind is tired of thinking or your body needs a break, it helps to do one of these things:

_____

_____

_____

_____

_____

_____

_____

_____

_____

_____

_____

_____

_____

_____

_____

_____

_____

_____

_____

_____

_____

_____

_____

CHAPTER 13

How to Use
Your Manual

Wow! You've made it this far, and you've done a lot of writing—you now have your very own owner's manual. Pat yourself on the back!

You have taken a huge step toward knowing yourself. The more you know, the more you can live the life you desire.

Refer to this manual to:

Make decisions
Remember who you are
Feel good about yourself
Work on things you indicated you wanted

Share this manual to:

Help someone know you better—whether it's a sibling, a parent, a friend, a partner. . . or a potential partner

Revisit and update this manual to:

Keep it fresh! Think of this manual as a living thing— ongoing and changing as you evolve

NOTES

Recommended: Every year or every few years, order a new blank book for updating.

Available in hard bound, paperback or as an ebook to print yourself. Go to www.balboapress.com or www.amazon.com.

Order additional owner's manuals for friends or loved ones!

Pat Hansen is a Certified Life Coach and Personal Branding Specialist who has a passion for living an authentic life. She studied design and communication at the University of Washington and the Kunst Gewerbeschule in Basel, Switzerland, and received her life coach certification from the Foundation for Holistic Life Coaching, founded by Alan Cohen. She lives on a small lake in Seattle, Washington, where she enjoys the water and abundant wildlife on a daily basis.

Comments, experiences, or results are welcome after using your owner's manual.

Life coaching appointments are available in-person, by phone, or using Skype.

Contact Pat at pathansenlifecoach@gmail.com or visit www.pathansenlifecoach.com.

Printed in the United States
by Baker & Taylor Publisher Services